COOL WHEELS

HIGH-SPEED SUPERBIKES

by Alan Dowds

GARETH**STEVENS**
GS
PUBLISHING
A Member of the WRC Media Family of Companies

Please visit our Web site at: www.garethstevens.com
For a free color catalog describing Gareth Stevens Publishing's
list of high-quality books and multimedia programs,
call 1-800-542-2595 (USA) or 1-800-387-3178 (Canada).
Gareth Stevens Publishing's fax: (414) 332-3567.

Library of Congress Cataloging-in-Publication Data

Dowds, Alan.
  High-speed superbikes / Alan Dowds.
      p. cm. — (Cool wheels)
  Includes bibliographical references and index.
  ISBN-10: 0-8368-6826-9 – ISBN-13: 978-0-8368-6826-5 (lib. bdg.)
  1. Superbikes—Juvenile literature. I. Title. II. Series
TL440.15.D69   2006
629.227'5—dc22   2006042296

This North American edition first published in 2007 by
Gareth Stevens Publishing
A Member of the WRC Media Family of Companies
330 West Olive Street, Suite 100
Milwaukee, WI 53212 USA

© 2006 Amber Books Ltd.

Produced by Amber Books Ltd., Bradley's Close,
74–77 White Lion Street, London N1 9PF, U.K.

Project Editor: Michael Spilling
Design: SOL
Picture Research: Terry Forshaw and Kate Green

Gareth Stevens editorial direction: Valerie J. Weber
Gareth Stevens editor: Jim Mezzanotte
Gareth Stevens art direction: Tammy West
Gareth Stevens cover design: Charlie Dahl
Gareth Stevens production: Jessica Morris

Picture credits: Mick. B: 5; Alan Dowds: 7, 11, 15, 19, 21, 23, 25, 29; Art-Tech/Aerospace: 9, 13;
Mac McDiarmid: 17; BMW: 27.

Artwork credits: DeAgostini: 4; Alex Pang (© Amber Books): 6, 16, 20, 24, 26; Amber Books: 8, 10;
Mark Franklin (© Amber Books): 12, 14, 18, 22, 28.

Printed in the United States of America

1 2 3 4 5 6 7 8 9 10 09 08 07 06

CONTENTS

KAWASAKI GPZ900R

The passenger seat is bigger and more comfortable than the seat on modern sports bikes.

The large square headlight was a very modern design in 1984.

The front **forks** have a special device to stop them from diving down when the brakes are applied.

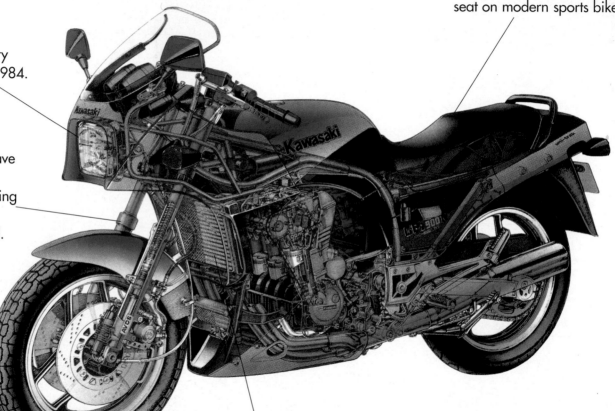

The **radiator** keeps the engine cool. Liquid flows past the **cylinders** and into the radiator. Passing wind then cools the liquid.

Left: With hard luggage cases, the GPZ900R makes a great bike for long-distance travel.

When the Kawasaki GPZ900R was first built in 1984, no other bike looked like it.

It was the most powerful sports bike at the time. The engine was cooled by liquid instead of air. It created a lot of **horsepower**.

A smooth **fairing** helped the bike cut through the air for greater speed.

The GPZ900R was so successful that it was still sold in Japan twenty years later, in 2004.

KAWASAKI GPZ 900R

First Year Made: 1984
Top Speed: 150 miles (241 km) per hour
Country: Japan
Power: 113.5 horsepower

DID YOU KNOW?

In 1984, GPZ900Rs competed in the British Isle of Man TT race for the first time. They came in first, second, and third!

HONDA CBR900RR FIREBLADE

The big **muffler** cuts down on noise from the engine.

Twin headlights help a rider see well at night.

Wide tires help the FireBlade grip the road.

The **swingarm** is made of lightweight **aluminum**.

This engine is an inline-four. It has four cylinders in a row. The engine sits sideways in the **frame**.

Honda's FireBlade is one of the most popular **superbikes** of all time. It first went on sale in 1992. At the time, it was faster and more powerful than most other bikes around. The Fireblade was the bike every young rider wanted to own.

Compact Power

The FireBlade is a lightweight superbike.

HONDA CBR900RR

First Year Made: 1992
Top Speed: 170 miles (274 km) per hour
Country: Japan
Power: 148 horsepower

Lighter bikes **accelerate** and slow down faster. They are also easier to turn than heavier bikes.

The CBR900RR is a small bike with an engine that is much bigger than other bikes of its size and weight. With its small size and powerful engine, the FireBlade is a fast, **nimble** bike. When it first came out, it could beat most other bikes on twisting, turning roads.

DID YOU KNOW?

Some people say the name "FireBlade" comes from a bad translation of the Japanese word for "lightning"!

DUCATI 916

The seat is designed for racing and is uncomfortable for long trips.

The front wheel has two **disc brakes**. They help stop the bike quickly.

A special swingarm connects the rear wheel to the frame.

This engine is a **liquid-cooled** V-twin. The two cylinders are arranged in a "V" shape.

Special tires grip the road well at high speed.

The Ducati 916 is one of the most beautiful motorcycles ever built.

Design Dream

Massimo Tamburini designed this superbike. He has created many fast motorcycles.

The bike's engine is narrow so Tamburini was able to create a slim bike that cuts through the air. Its shape helps it reach high speeds

DUCATI 916

First Year Made: 1993
Top Speed: 170 miles (274 km) per hour
Country: Italy
Power: 107.5 horsepower

without a huge amount of power.

The 916 has twin mufflers under the seat. It has a special rear **suspension**, too.

Quick Change

Most swingarms hold the rear wheel on both sides. The swingarm on the 916, however, only holds it on the left side. If you look at the bike on the other side, the wheel seems to be unattached, or "floating"! This design is unusual, but it makes changing the rear wheel easier and quicker.

DID YOU KNOW?

The Ducati 916 has been very successful in racing. Carl Fogarty, an English racer, won the World Superbike Championship four times on his Ducati — in 1994, 1995, 1998, and 1999.

MV AGUSTA F4 750

The steel-tube frame is light and strong.

The front suspension forks are much thicker than most bikes.

The small engine is tilted forward.

Big **calipers** grab the disks for quick stops.

Left: MV Agusta won an amazing seventy-five world championships in the second half of the twentieth century.

MV AGUSTA F4 750

First Year Made: 1999
Top Speed: 175 miles (282 km) per hour
Country: Italy
Power: 132 horsepower

The MV Agusta F4 750 was designed by Massimo Tamburini, who also created the Ducati 916. This Italian superbike gets its name from its four-cylinder engine. The F4 is the only four-cylinder bike made in Italy. The Italian carmaker Ferrari helped design the engine, which is very powerful for its size.

DID YOU KNOW?

Agusta is an Italian company. It used to make helicopters as well as motorcycles.

SUZUKI GSX1300R HAYABUSA

Two large scoops feed air to the engine for more power.

The **exhaust** goes through two large mufflers, one on each side of the bike.

Holes in the front brake disks help keep them cool and save weight.

The Hayabusa's back tire is very tough, so it can handle high-speed use.

When the Suzuki GSX1300R Hayabusa first appeared in 1999, it was the fastest bike in the world. It has a very powerful four-cylinder engine.

Superfast Cruiser

Besides its huge power, the bike also has a large fairing and windshield, to help it move smoothly through the air. The

Left: Although the Hayabusa is a large bike, it handles well, even on tight corners.

SUZUKI GSX1300R HAYABUSA

First Year Made: 1999
Top Speed: 198 miles (319 km) per hour
Country: Japan
Power: 172.5 horsepower

Hayabusa can reach speeds of almost 200 miles (320 km) per hour.

The bike's brakes and suspension were designed for traveling at high speeds. The bike can stop quickly and smoothly, even when it is traveling very fast.

The Hayabusa is a large, heavy bike, but it handles well. It is good for fast cruising!

DID YOU KNOW?

The Hayabusa is named after a Japanese falcon. This bird can travel almost 200 miles (320 km) per hour when diving for prey.

KAWASAKI ZX-12R

The ZX-12R has an unusual hollow frame. The battery and air cleaner are inside this frame.

The large scoop below the headlights lets in air for the engine.

The rear tire on the ZX-12R is 7.8 inches (20 centimeters) wide. It is as wide as some car tires.

Valves let fuel and air into the cylinders.

When Kawasaki first introduced the ZX-12R, in 1999, it was the fastest and most powerful superbike in the world.

Its engine has smaller cylinders than similar bikes, such as the Suzuki Hayabusa, but the ZX-12R makes more horsepower.

The engine has a more modern, **efficient** design. It does a better job of creating power

Left: Although designed as a road bike, the ZX-12R has the speed and handling to compete on the track.

than other engines.

Fastest in Its Class

The ZX-12R is also more **aerodynamic** than other bikes of its size. It can cut through the air more easily, so

it goes faster. It is also lighter. The ZX-12R is good for short trips on winding roads. It has a small seat, however, so it is not comfortable for long journeys.

KAWASAKI ZX-12R

First Year Made: 1999
Top Speed: 190 miles (306 km) per hour
Country: Japan
Power: 187.5 horsepower

DID YOU KNOW?

Kawasaki calls all its sports bikes "Ninjas," after the legendary Japanese warriors of the past.

TRIUMPH BONNEVILLE

The flat seat provides plenty of room for the rider and a passenger.

The Bonneville has wire-spoke wheels, like many older bikes.

The chrome-plated exhaust pipes are called "peashooters" because of their shape.

The **air-cooled** engine has two cylinders side-by-side.

16

Triumph Bonnevilles were first made in 1959. Although the modern version looks similar to the old one, it has a slightly larger engine and many improvements.

A Modern Bike

The new Bonneville has a more modern engine and **chassis** than the first models. The new engine is much more

TRIUMPH BONNEVILLE

First Year Made: 1959
Top Speed: 120 miles (193 km) per hour
Country: United Kingdom
Power: 60 horsepower

powerful and less likely to break down. With its new chassis, the bike handles better, so it can reach high speeds more safely.

The new Bonneville has better brakes. It is safer to handle on corners and on wet, slippery roads. The front forks and rear **shock absorbers** have an old look, but they are a brand new design.

People who loved the old bike can now ride a modern Bonneville with all of the style of the old one.

DID YOU KNOW?

The Bonneville is named after the Bonneville Salt Flats in Utah, where many speed records have been set.

YAMAHA FZ-1 1000

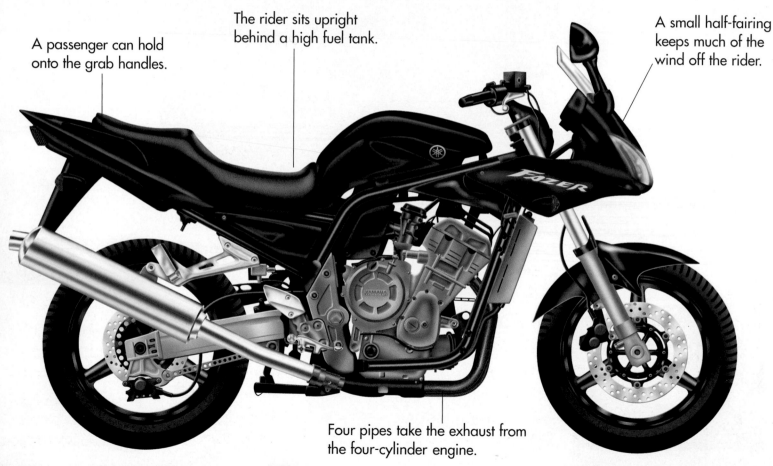

A passenger can hold onto the grab handles.

The rider sits upright behind a high fuel tank.

A small half-fairing keeps much of the wind off the rider.

Four pipes take the exhaust from the four-cylinder engine.

The Yamaha FZ-1 is a lightweight road bike with the power of a superbike.

It has a racing-style engine, taken from the Yamaha YZF-R1, but it also has a road bike chassis that gives a comfortable ride.

Everyday Power

Although it has a very powerful four-cylinder engine, the FZ-1 is much

Left: The FZ-1's upright riding position and small fairing make it a very comfortable bike to ride.

YAMAHA FZ-1

First Year Made: 2000
Top Speed: 160 miles (257 km) per hour
Country: Japan
Power: 143 horsepower

smaller and lighter than most superbikes. It is designed for comfort, so it is good both for long journeys and everyday riding.

Yamaha has also given this bike powerful racing brakes and a strong suspension. It is an exciting bike to ride on twisting turns.

DID YOU KNOW?

In the United States, this bike is called the FZ-1. In other parts of the world, it is called the "Fazer."

HARLEY-DAVIDSON V-ROD

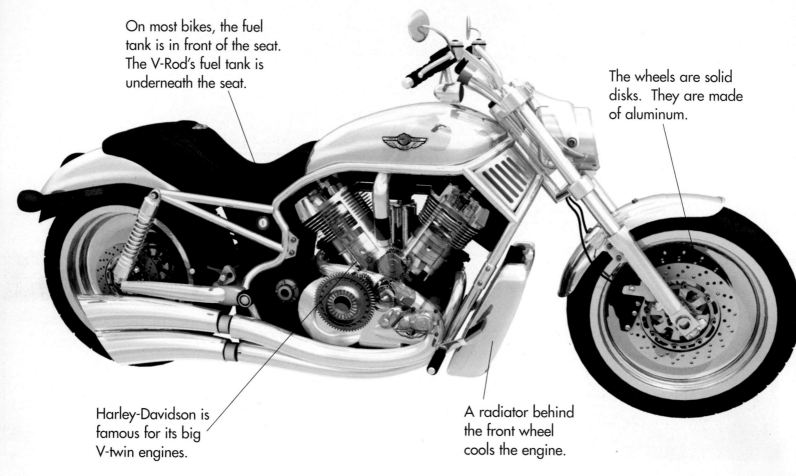

On most bikes, the fuel tank is in front of the seat. The V-Rod's fuel tank is underneath the seat.

The wheels are solid disks. They are made of aluminum.

Harley-Davidson is famous for its big V-twin engines.

A radiator behind the front wheel cools the engine.

Harley-Davidson bikes were first built in the 1890s. The V-Rod is one of the company's most modern motorcycle designs.

The engine is liquid-cooled instead of air-cooled, like older Harley-Davidson designs. The engine is taken from Harley Davidson's AMA (American Motorcyclist Association) race bike, the VR1000. It is a

HARLEY DAVIDSON V-ROD

First Year Made: 2001
Top Speed: 135 miles (217 km) per hour
Country: United States
Power: 113 horsepower

powerful engine that uses **fuel injection**.

Comfortable Cruiser

The bike has a very low seat, forward-mounted footpegs, and high handlebars. A rider sits back on the bike, making it a very comfortable street cruiser.

The bike was designed for performance, too. The tires and brakes are similar to those used on sports bikes.

DID YOU KNOW?

The V-Rod's fuel tank is under the seat, so the rider has to flip the seat up to get at the fuel cap.

BUELL FIREBOLT XB12R

The engine turns a rubber belt. This belt then turns the rear wheel.

A small fairing protects the rider from the wind.

The muffler is below the engine so that it will not scrape on the road when riders lean over in turns.

The engine has fins to keep it cool.

Buell is a company that makes sports bikes using Harley-Davidson engines.

Smart Racer

The engine in the Firebolt XB12R is a V-twin. It has two cylinders in the shape of a "V." The engine is air-cooled. It has many ridges on the outside, called fins. Air cools these fins.

BUELL FIREBOLT XB12R

First Year Made: 2003
Top Speed: 145 miles (233 km) per hour
Country: United States
Power: 99 horsepower

Left: The small Buell Firebolt XB12R is good on twisting roads because it handles corners well.

DID YOU KNOW?

The Firebolt does not have a separate fuel tank. Instead, the fuel is kept inside the frame, which is hollow.

The frame is made of aluminum. Many bikes have two disk brakes in front. The Firebolt has one big brake, to save weight. It also has a short **wheelbase**, so it can change direction quickly. It is good on winding roads.

HONDA CBR600RR

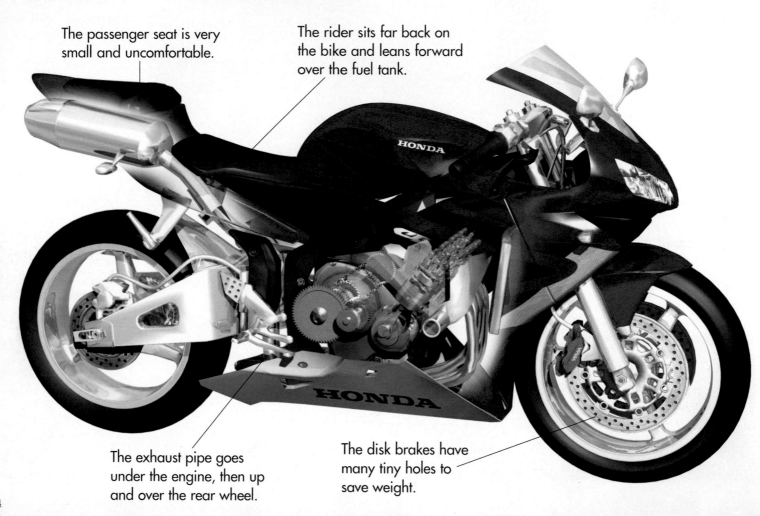

The passenger seat is very small and uncomfortable.

The rider sits far back on the bike and leans forward over the fuel tank.

The exhaust pipe goes under the engine, then up and over the rear wheel.

The disk brakes have many tiny holes to save weight.

The Honda CBR600RR is one of the most successful bikes of its size. Since it was first made in 2003, it has been popular with both racers and people who ride on regular roads.

Racing Model

The RR version has a very sporty design. Early models had more comfortable seats and taller fairings, but the

Left: Riders can lean this bike way over on sharp corners. The muffler is up high, so it will not hit the ground in corners.

RR is designed for the racetrack. The engine is very small and powerful, and the frame is both light and strong.

The CBR600RR is a very successful race bike. It has been first across the finish line in many races around the world. The bike won the Supersport World Championship from 2003 to 2005.

HONDA CBR600RR

First Year Made: 2003
Top Speed: 165 miles (266 km) per hour
Country: Japan
Power: 113 horsepower

DID YOU KNOW?

Honda is the largest engine maker in the world. It makes engines for cars, boats, and lawnmowers, as well as for motorcycles.

BMW K1200R

A bracket holds the muffler in place.

The headlights are oval-shaped.

The K1200R has a single shock absorber above the front wheel.

This bike has a steel shaft instead of a chain. The engine spins the shaft, which turns the back wheel.

Antilock brakes keep the bike from skidding on wet or icy roads.

The BMW K1200R is a very fast bike. It has a powerful engine, so it can accelerate quickly and reach high speeds. The liquid-cooled engine has four cylinders.

Chassis Design

Unlike most powerful bikes, it does not have a large fairing to protect the rider from the wind. At high speeds, the rider

Left: The K1200R is a powerful bike. It is good for both racing and traveling on regular roads.

BMW K1200R

First Year Made: 2005
Top Speed: 165 miles (266 km) per hour
Country: Germany
Power: 165 horsepower

must hold on tight to avoid being blown off!

The K1200R has an unusual chassis design. The front suspension has just one shock absorber above the front wheel. Most bikes have two shock absorbers in front, inside the forks on either side of the wheel.

DID YOU KNOW?

BMW stands for "Bavarian Motor Works." It is based in Munich, Germany. The company is also well known for making luxury cars and sports cars.

TRIUMPH DAYTONA 650

The frame and suspension are made of aluminum, which is light and strong.

The Daytona comes in three colors — bright red, gray, and yellow.

The hole below the headlights brings air to the engine to cool it.

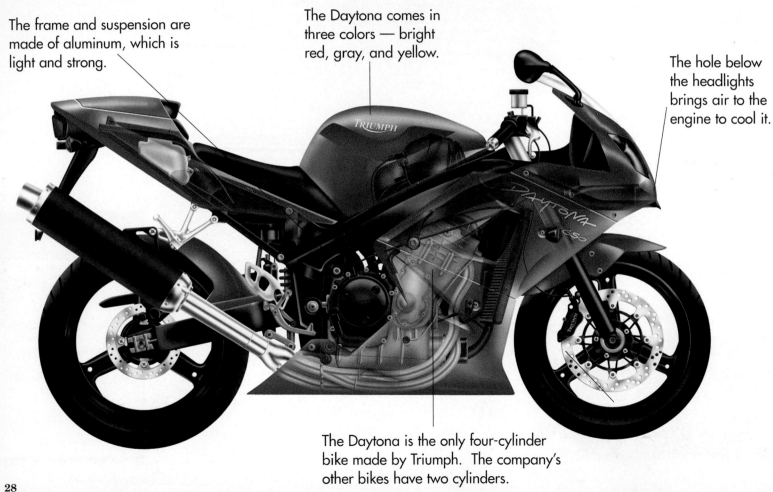

The Daytona is the only four-cylinder bike made by Triumph. The company's other bikes have two cylinders.

The Triumph Daytona 650 is named after the Daytona Speedway, a racetrack in Florida.

This Daytona model is based on the Daytona 600. Its engine is larger by 50 cubic centimeters (3 cubic inches). The 650 is faster than the smaller, less powerful 600. It can keep up with other bikes that are similar to it, such as the Honda CBR600RR.

TRIUMPH DAYTONA 650

First Year Made: 2005
Top Speed: 160 miles (257 km) per hour
Country: United Kingdom
Power: 111 horsepower

Fuel Injection

The 650 has a four-cylinder engine and a computer-controlled fuel injection system. The computer decides how much fuel to feed the engine, so the bike goes faster without using a lot more fuel. This computer also helps cut down on exhaust, which is harmful to the environment.

DID YOU KNOW?

The Daytona 650 did not sell very well, so Triumph replaced it with a three-cylinder version in 2006.

GLOSSARY

air-cooled — a term describing an engine that uses air flowing past it to keep from getting too hot.

accelerate — increase in speed.

aerodynamic — having a shape that slips easily through the air.

aluminum — a strong, lightweight metal.

antilock brakes — brakes with a device that keeps them from locking up when a rider slows down quickly.

calipers — the part of a disc brake that squeezes the disk, slowing the wheel.

chassis — the frame and suspension of a motorcycle.

cylinders — spaces inside an engine where fuel and air explode to create power.

disc brakes — a braking system in which calipers on a vehicle squeeze discs attached to the wheels.

efficient — able to do something without wasting energy.

exhaust — the gases an engine creates when it burns fuel and air.

fairing — a covering on the front and sides of a motorcycle that make it more aerodynamic and protect the rider.

forks — on a motorcycle, the metal tubes on either side of the front wheel that connect it to the frame.

frame — the part of a motorcycle that supports the engine, suspension, and rider.

fuel injection — a system that sprays fuel into an engine.

horsepower — the amount of power an engine produces, based on how much work one horse can do.

liquid-cooled — a term describing an engine that uses liquid flowing around the cyclinders to keep from getting too hot.

muffler — the part of a motorcycle that keeps down noise when exhaust leaves the engine.

nimble — able to move around quickly.

radiator — a device used with a liquid-cooled engine. It cools the liquid that flows around the cylinders, keeping the engine from getting too hot.

shock absorbers — devices that keep a motorcycle from bouncing too much when going over bumps.

superbikes — high-performance motorcycles that are often designed for racing.

suspension — the parts that attach the wheels to a motorcycle and help it ride smoothly on bumpy surfaces.

swingarm — a long arm that connects the rear wheel to the frame of a motorcycle.

wheelbase — the distance between the front and rear wheels, measured from where each wheel touches the ground.

FOR MORE INFORMATION

Books

Motorbike Racing. Action Sports (series).
Tony Norman (Gareth Stevens Publishing)

Motorbikes. Mean Machines (series).
Mark Morris (Raintree)

Motorbikes. Transport Around the World (series).
Chris Oxlade (Heinemann Educational Books)

Motorbikes. World's Greatest (series).
Ian Graham (Raintree)

Motorcycles. Race Car Legends (series).
Jeff Savage (Chelsea House)

Super Bikes. Monster Machines (series).
David Jefferis (Raintree)

Web Sites

American Motorcycle Association
www.ama-cycle.org

The Antique Motorcycle Club of America
www.antiquemotorcycle.org

Bikesters: An Adventure in Racing and Technology
www.bikesters.com

Honda Racing
www.hondaredriders.com

INDEX